Vacationland

Ander Monson

TP

TUPELO PRESS

First paperback edition May 2005
Library of Congress Control Number 2004114637

Tupelo Press
PO Box 539, Dorset, Vermont 05251
802.366.8185 • Fax 802.362.1883
editor@tupelopress.org • web www.tupelopress.org

Cover and text designed by William Kuch, WK Graphic Design

All for Megan,
one way back.

TABLE OF CONTENTS

THREE

Maybe there is a way beyond the winter and the weather: less directed elegies and love poems

ONE

*For Jesse,
so long
gone*

SALT

It covers everything, a glossy January rind
along tires. Sunny days have brought it out
burned away the ice, left
calcified tidelines to gloat
on the hoods and sun-warm trunks
of cars queued up along the curb,
parking close as they can get
to each other, to the raised
sidewalk that's buried
beneath the dirt crust next to the neon-lit
sign for the funeral home.

The body of the boy we knew is still
inside, the cheeks teased
back to cheery life with rouge.

The ice on the canal
the faulty floor through which he descended
blazing on the back of his Arctic Cat
is black as slate
which means it's thin
and boys on the shore
throw aimless stones that yield
ricochets with laser sounds.

The outdoor rink is bare, festooned
with bits of the Canadian flag
fragments of the maple leaf
glistening starlike after storm.

INVENTORY ELEGY 1:
A Paper Remnant

- dead skull ember
- cat's eye marble thumbed to a heart
- ambergris; amber
- handmade paper snowflake char
- tin sliver buried in a toe
- pop tops gathered from aluminum cans for sex
- one zipper hip boot, gone solo
- graffiti rubbed out on a desk
- half-filled bottles of Corona
- pink lady slippers cut and pressed
- aurora, aureole
- gas can fume, dispersed
- wisp sugar caked on a stick
- lockpick

ENTRY-LEVEL ELEGY

One is gone, we know; now
the one we know is gone. And so
a position has opened up in the line
we stand in every night to jump
off the bridge and into something like excitement;
we queue so as to avoid an aerial collision
so no one goes half-assed
and all auto-accident then gone on us.

The son of the university
president is dead. We feel like chicken
wire. And setting fire to things.
And nothing will ever be the same—
not the car-sized flag that towers
over Perkins, or the phoned-in threats
to bomb the school in lieu of showing up
for tests we knew we'd fail.

Not the smell of newspaper ink on hands
stained from weeks of examining obituaries,
not the sutures stinging in my arm
where they just excised the tumor.

The future is a shoulder
without the promise of an arm.

You know how this goes.
The litany of cars like ants
in the picnic and funeral procession
will never gleam the same
or issue the same exhaust.

Even the sun is done for the season.

Juvenile delinquents, preoccupied,
spray-paint your name on overpasses
instead of those of girls they shun
but dream about.

Even the shotgunned *Welcome to etc.*
signs in the little towns
that clot around the river
seem to read your name
then: *Population 0. Recently unincorporated.*

I guess this is where I enter grief,
with a hand on a salt lick
and reeking of beer they don't
even make anymore. Wear a shirt
that looks like a sack, a fresh hat, and great pants
to the funeral.

This is where you come in too,
Herr reader, accidental deer-killer
in the intermittently-headlit night
(what could you have done?), lotus-eater,
each word each line a kind
of draught, a telegraph of my intentions:
forgetfulness and whatever is left
of the moon as it wanes,

bad eighties songs like "Home Sweet Home"
intermittent on the radio,
or anything by Warrant,
some miniature-golf-sized magic
against remembering
too long, too clearly, or not at all.

AFTER YOU'VE GONE ON AND THROUGH

Loose buoys drift like bobbers
hooked into the backs of mallard ducks.

Slow boats coil across the canal, inscribing
vees; their wakes fan out, amalgamate

with tepid rainbow peels
the remains of gasoline

saucy on the water. No one
is eloping; the air is stopped with smoke

from controlled burn.
Bodies are interred on shore.

A sousaphone
like a huge white snail

laments beside a grave, and nothing
has a purpose, the reverend complains

while mourners hack
into gleaming handkerchiefs, their hearts

removed. Blue-hatted ladies
opine behind the crowd, aloof.

Topiary gardeners clip discreetly
inside the maze of swelling hedges.

Tree inspectors crowd the street
with their negotiations,

mark which boughs to cut,
which are singing with disease.

They call the city contractors
who will come to trim

according to the yellow mark.
Anesthesiologists

and surgeons in their scrubs and masks
in fluorescent-lighted operating rooms

finger bone saws, the tools to use
to prune those limbs

when they're deafened
beyond repair.

THINGS COME UP

Snow dust around the trolling blades of plows;
sometimes sparks when the road is clear of ice,
is bright with recent salt; new advances
in geometry (hint: not much has changed)
in a conversation with a former
teacher. Rocks heaved through the Sleeman greenhouse

glass have caused a mess of speculation.
Michigan Bell trucks robbed of equipment,
their windows smashed in too. Everyone has
a trashed glass story, says not to worry,
this vacationland is safe, is no more
rife with the TV threat of gangs come up

like threat from cities South and myth of here:
Green Bay, Bad Axe, Pontiac, Detroit, Flint.

ASTONISH

If the work of rock is shift & chip & fault,
then the work of fingertip along neck
is good and well-deserved; then asphalt can
astonish us by going soft in back
of Festival Foods, where the bears' Friday
night dumpster-dive for trash & strew & mess
is entertainment for us this far north.
Asphalt's slumming, slurring under sun is
some work too. If what we call a road is
no more solid than a Shamrock Shake thrown
out, reclining in the trash; if what we
call the ground is hurtle, globe, then we are
breakneck, roller coaster gone, or famished
from lack of love, finishing & finished.

ALIBI

It's a sieve, your story in the Gazette,
a gutty lattice of motions and motivations,
your glittering flippers castigating the net.
Where were you the night of Y
were you with Liz my X
whom I always dreamed I loved
and could never get
what had you drunk
where had you gone
etc.

Machines vend bait
and line the streets. Grim and grinning,
they summon me. In the day
after your death, a dollar buys a half-pound
of earthworm, leech, or fluke. Styrofoam tubs
continue to contain nickels
and lead slugs for weight
and the dried french onion
worm remains.

The too-smooth moon
continues to pursue
its solemn cliché above.
Its pull on the lake is slight
but undiminished.

I think intermittently
of your knuckles on the clutch
the deep crease your body made in the seat
the whole way down. I see you in strobe
in scenes of resignation and fear,
the emotional clutter of descent,
then you—still très cool—in the litter
of skeletal pines, some still strung out
with lights—their secondhand hymns
mumming below the water line.

The divers tie warning-orange flags
to the snowmobile, claim number printed
indelible in ink. The license tags are noted
and your husk is roped in and up. The corpus
rises slowly—as all good things do,
and seems to reactivate, kicking in the current—
to flashbulbs, removal, and the levy
of funeral and interment taxes.

When did we begin to affix
the arc of myth to your descent,
you Orpheus, you Icarus
you hot puck, you skate
you stick-battered dog?
You dumb doldrum tympan
you skin of a man
you muskellunge fisher
you prized and glorious ham
you study hall king
you meniscus?

You can cremate me when I go through
jack my ashes in a plastic fashion buoy
no name, date, or epitaph. I'll pass
on the grandeur and all the sunny claims
the lemon bars crowned with sugar,
the tongues lashing at the lips
at the after-funeral feast.
There will be no one to love or to expel.

Your pass, though dumb as light, and filled
with the most terrifying sort of love,
depressed a button, left the gas
milling in the stove, the lathe
gently whirring in the shop,
the water filling in the basement,
the pilot burning like a laxative
dreaming, roaming, *ing*-ing
inaction eternally in action at the wheel

ELEGY ANALOGY I

THE BOY you knew
who went through the ice

is to

YOUR COMPLICITY in his disappearance

as:

a.   hacked-up : fixed
b.   your guilt : your scorn
c.   to take heart : make a fist
d.   to mourn : take form
e.   to need : enliven
f.   the ether : the knife
g.   to knead : to unleaven
h.   the hole : the coal
i.   barges miles out on the lake : how they list
j.   to take the word from stone : bring it home
k.   the petal : the pistil
l.   the womb : the bomb
m.   to watch : to desert
n.   to write it : to deserve it

GOLD AND SOMEONE (FLASHBACK)

Canyon Falls, one descent among many
and maybe the ones since less spectacular
or more, into Lou Reed singing "Heroin"
and throwing bolt lightning
across pool hall smoke-dark tables,
and failures that were there to be trod upon
and left. This one's marked with the wash
of shifting stations from the Chevette
stationed in the lot next to the road
that leads down to the so-blue lake
so it looks like you're descending
into swimming pool or sky.

The radio's no good, can't hold a signal.
And you hold no grudge against the dentist's son
in front of you in spite of tools applied
over afternoons of major reconstruction and fluoride
paste, lead jackets worn to protect you
from fluorescent sun, bad music, a sincere case of halitosis,
and some kind of laser bullshit rays.

What's invisible cannot be counted,
cannot count against your liver or your bones.
This is your theory delivered *sotto voce*
while we wait in line to jump, that enough calcium in milk
will keep your back straight, will keep the cars warm
and the radios on with their sonic deltas flooding out the night.

And in momentary flashlight light
you are struck with gold and someone
thinks of you a year away and that colossal moss
that lives in Michigan which you cut a piece from
and diminished.

Your living is a wick, and the heat
curlicuing up from your new flat-top,
just barber-given, is a trace of future light
and remonstrance, wax remainder, shift,

and your departure is a fraying hem,
too thin to hold a song or ache,
a disappointment whistler
bottle rocket dud—

not this particular departure
as you sound off a makeshift "Hey"
and arm wheel out in space in spite
of gravity like in cartoons watched
in black and white on old TVs,
then down into the pool below
as everyone is warm in laughter and cigarettes,
the possible beginnings of pneumonia,
and illuminating lighter flick,

but that necessary going
that is too soon—we know
or think we've heard—to come.

EXCISION

Photographs of you through the ice
the black and whites in the Gazette
of your machine being craned
up from the canal.

Here's one of ice like a scar
that has to be cracked back open
like a car crash windshield
fixed in the night.

Kids on the bridge.
The body's return
on a gurney. Its skin not blue
but dark like a bruise.
A shot of the shroud.

The paper's smell
of oil and ink.

One of the boil on the ice,
the gap, the wet gate
from a cancerous life
of bars, dull adrenaline
haze, and drunken
punches taken in the chest
like shots, a convenient job
at the Citgo station
selling liquor to teens.

A route out, one of few.

When is incision necessary to unzip the skin,
clear the way for removal? When
does a mole fatten, go oblique
like a ship or shocked whale,
turn lesion, tumor, malignant?
When must it be cut, burned, or frozen
whatever the cost to the body?

CELEBRITY

Why do we claim your celebrity,
coming only as it did with your winter
death? In February, after the memorial service—
though not the burial, which won't come until
spring when the ground's warm as milk or epidermis—
we clot outside the church, form groves
against the wind, and pass your name around
like a plate. Mrs. Des Rochers—the obligatory
blue-haired lady with the spot on her head in the shape of Elvis
Costello or Jesus—wants us to believe she's been crying
but we all know better, the shared wisdom of the town
and of the winter moving through us like a charge,
like we had all joined hands to make a chain
and the one on each end would reach
to the electric mouth of the hand dryer
shiny in the men's bathroom on the first floor
of the old Houghton High School building
that's now a cluttered ruin. You'd huck your voice
around in class like you would a hoop
and get us all to move with you
to the bathroom, no spit-dirty chickens now
to put our mettle to your test. How
if we all held hands, that lusty electric mix
would assure and course right through us
like you coursed through the ice
and down through the lake
until you reflected off the bottom
in your one great flash bulb
terror of a moment
and maybe we would see your face
scouring the bottom of the ice
like curlers with their brushes do
or cartoonish talk show guests, elbowing
the inside curve of the television screen
and when one of us broke the electric link,
we'd all feel the jolt that was, I thought, like birth
or death, a shock and something forceful, new.

SUMMER IS A MYSTERY IN MICHIGAN

Daylight, axelight, belltoll: all gone long. What blood
comes packaged in the mail. What unexpected summer hail
descends, suspended in the air. What hairlengths
are stranded on my chair like twine, or mines. What abandoned wine-

dark sea can we hear through the storm glass pane,
what cheap brand of wine is breathing in the fridge,
what ledge on which we're perched, what whirlpool
turning counterclockwise in the Sturgeon river,

what brand of pizza is delivered, what number
that we call to have our food arrive on time, what steam
coming off it in the doorway—in which the door is missing—
what drizzling pissing sound of rain, what ant-assembled

mound we found below your parents' rented cabin porch,
what torch we burned to keep the bugs haloed around us.

COMMISERATE

Be guaranteed by grief's long warranty
that you will always be able to return
to this: fresh sense of absence as a sort of fix,
one tunnel through the snow wall,

one finger insinuated into the veil,
a reassurance of your position
in isolation, opposite the mourners
who wax their legs and remonstrate

outside the church. The architecture
of their discussion is balsa, faulty,
with the very cheapest nails.
Everyone comes thin with smiles

on rails and solaces of steaming food—
green bean hotdish for the potluck,
sugar frosted lemon bars, that mustard-
egg-and-mushroom composition

that Mrs. Vivien always brings
and takes home untouched,
then brings again. Her persistence
is so winning that you become a fan

and, regardless of its turmeric
signature on your funeral gown,
allow yourself to eat and be consoled,
no matter how full you say you are.

VACATIONLAND

The Vacationland Motel's swimming pool is filled
with dread and droppings, wings of desiccated bugs.
They refuse to hum and fill the air with that peculiar music.

The oldest fish in the world looms underneath the lake.
We drain our drinks, think of smelt, and set
the tumblers on the table that is made of frosted glass
where they will leave rings behind like angel skins or sickness.

My brother clucks his tongue at me.

Dad is in the woods behind;
you can tell by the pines' parting motion
and that smell of work and blood and dog.

A woman wanders by with bags on her hands,
says nothing. She reeks of pitch and gristle.

Meat scent suggests a nearby grill.

Early evening stars are colander holes
through which the sky drains out.

This is the year where we define deceased.

TWO

For Liz,
that X and
then forever,
and for some
others, too

PROPRIETARY ELEGY

Start here & this one's mine: geometric
car glass leftover from the wreck,
a crust in a casserole dish
so baked-on it's dark and hard

as tar, and just as tough to scrape
or separate; possible absolution for my wish
for Jesse's death just a week
before it happened.

I am responsible for this glaze, this mess
I guess, this depression constellation,
this electric pinprick wash
of missives misfired from the nerves

of the just-woke leg or half-lit brain.
Imagine if it never woke again—became
a work, a heaviness I'd drag around, a backpack
filled with stars the size and heft

of hearts, dwarf-colored, the scraped-
off skins of artichokes, old-smoke-
filled vacuum glass, those thoughts
of Liz my X my melting point

my onliness, my creak & ache
my gone & buried in the lake—
those needlepoints in skin, her name
x 5, those good-for-little loose tattoos.

INVENTORY ELEGY 2:
Your Grandma Sent You Gum In Letters

- desiccated sticks of Doublemint
- watermark and ink
- brave pocket lint
- tire skid and brake
- slow descent of starlight
- strong feeling about crime
- season, long and white
- bad alibi
- gear that could be star
- comparison to Rayon
- X (or loss thereof) which is endured
- consternation
- night without your fingertip anomaly
- keyhole memory; empty inquiry

APPROXIMATION

The coroner's best guess as to time of death
is sometime in the earliness
before the light has staked its claim
with hammer-blows and useless threats of ice
spilled like perfume across roads.

As for the cause, you know it's notoriously
iffy—in this case, safe to say, death
by drowning or by impact of the cheek
against the windshield, against the radio dial
which left its mark, or death due
to after-prom excitement—the occasion
marked by streamers in the rafters
and the crowning of the school's best
heads and shoulders with a tin foil
wrapped, fake-bejeweled band.

Death due to lack of the right date
who might have taken the right route
to the after party, who might not have swerved
to miss the fish—the stiff enigma,
a frozen trout in the middle of the lane,
the body like a beacon
a warning of the impending season's weakness,
of after-graduation life in bars
and doldrum rum and cokes in glasses.

Death due to lack of escapist training,
no Houdini present, no Tupac, Elvis
surviving death at least in myth
and continuing to release
themselves in beats & language
to increasing critical suspicion.

Death due to loneliness
and books checked out too long ago
from the Public Library
and not returned on time,
death due to accruing, reoccurring fines
that continued to mount like banks of snow
until she returned them on prom night

until I went to check them out again
to have her signature—some vestige
of her neck / her mind / her hands.

I AM GETTING SERIOUS ABOUT GRIEF

I load his old bones into the bed
of the orange GMC that rusted in half
before we could give it a proper
shotgun funeral. You've heard of weddings
like this. Or wakes, where grief is enforced
and impossible. Where ladies stir
their gin drinks with sticks
and you want to slide out
like sleep from a drunk.

Where the lilies are still-lives.

His beer-making kit is still in the cellar
where the yeast is in packets
and the walls' grape stink
doesn't sweeten. I keep salamanders
here and grow sprouts in wet jars.

What else is there to do? It's turkey-
day and liquor-cold. A rabbit
nailed to a tree
on the road up to the house
is singing. It's really something
awful.

Grackles line the electric wires
that keep me lit with this world.
I cut words from the paper,
stash them in sacks. Bury
them under the house
with artichoke hearts
where everything is clay.

I pull clams
from the lake with my hands
and rinse them into a pail.
I am old. I don't know
enough about shellfish
to know which ones have pearls
and which just hold hooks or bits
of line, or are filled with grit,
as if that weren't enough.

STILL LIFE WITH HALF OF WALTER MITTY

Retain the good and sullen parts in lye
and let the dreaming leak and stew in jars.
We have his torso like Apollo's husk
taxidermied, hung above the mantel
where all good things are full and stiff and fixed:
several generations' thumbs, a tacked-up
sun facsimile, my botched shop cutting
board project: a pineapple or a bomb,
a collar or a tourniquet slipped down
through generations, hockey stick once used
by Bobby Orr with whom my cousins played
which still exhibits blood as fast as trace
or thunderhead, resists the light like song
or black sap tolling gong-like from a trunk.

MY GRANDFATHER'S THUMB

Like my dad's,
it floats in the jar
on the mantel,
aloft in cooking oil.

Like the hummingbirds
that orbit the feeder,
desperate for nectar
that we purchase in the bottle
from the hardware store
and sometimes lace with Comet
or Mr. Clean
when my brother
is particularly grim.

Like the necks of just-hacked chickens,
or stars in air around the freshly-dead,

It is both ember and emblem of loss,

An appendix,
the vestige in the body,

the fishing lure caught
and resonating in the eye,

the register of the disturbance
of ancestry and necessity.

The remaining
family hands
nicked with cuts
pitched up to the
cooling, killing
moon.

BURN, BURN

Burn for X, for loss, for burning itself,
for the mantra that repeats / swings like a bell
in a cage in the tower that hasn't had use's grease
for hours but continues to toll,
extolling its maker, extolling the movement of air
through the window that looks like a cross.

Burn down the wall that keeps us from the river.

Burn down the stop sign that keeps cars from bursting into the
    intersection.

Let fire's grace take it all and convert it to gas
and also to ash and to char
that will move in the air for years before settling.

Burn down the barn crushed under snow
when it melts and the frame dries enough
to go up without trouble.

Reduce it to rubble, to ruin, home base for the chipmunks
that leave stitch-marks on the snow crust
after the sun has crisped it and left it to cool.

Subtract this from X,
from the hole in the ice on the skin of the lake,
from the scar left by retrieval,

Subtract this from substrate and glistening masses
of just-below-the-surface rock
that will no longer bring profit to the mines
and the companies that employ the men
who dark their lungs for them by day.

ELEGY FOR LUGGAGE

Only one container filled with residual words and old air.
The others: luggage, cheery print boxers from the Gap,
and clothes involving straps and buckles,
goldfish cooled in plastic bags
tied inside Ziploc freezer keepers. Tubes of iodine and cork-
stopped jars of turmeric. Frozen pints of blood in styrofoam
wrapped in sheet music to keep them singing.

Everything is an airport, is stained
like an airport, has to be lived through like an airport—
visible through the scrub blind and clean, the air spiteful, luke-
warm, an operating room for travel and regret.

The Detroit Metro E-gate wing
where the short-hop planes mass and wait
has had enough of loss. Men in queues, eyes lit by momentary sex,
slide wedding bands into pockets. Men on the patch
sit at the smokeless *Cheers* franchise
in lint-rolled chamois shirts,
admonish each other, exfoliate their pricey drinks. Some chums
reminisce and pat each others' thighs.
Thieves troll the baggage claim for leftovers,
abandoned Samsonites with flimsy silver locks.
Voices Scheherazade in air to keep their loves
from leaving, and we are waiting for an urn
to arrive on the automatic belt
through the plastic flaps. Some of us have violence
in our hearts. Others, departure. Some confess
under fluorescent lights. The snow outside trails down
from hammer-clouds, old and vague machines,
precipitation backlit from street bulbs,
some darkened by pellet guns,
some idly burning targets.

CONTINGENCY ELEGY

If I grieve by default
when someone has gone through
and leaves a halo in the ice
where the water has stitched up
its own soundless wound

*

If all there is is silence after

If all there is is suppose Train A
leaves Memphis and Train B
leaves Memphis
how far apart are they when

*

If all there is is denominator
operand & the answers
to the even questions
in the back

*

If all there is is fill in
the blank with black mark
and spackle BAD, ABBA, ABACAB
in the same old ovals

*

If all there is is tomb and sulking

*

If all there is is what is printed in the papers

*

If all there is is silk from rafters

*

If all there is is food congealing on a table

*

If streamers always stream
& sentences meant to end
with question marks do not

*

If a halo is like a mouth but brighter

*

If, more specific, now: Liz's mouth
is like a halo
both are kissable
and lipgloss sound
when applied to lips is good

*

If the school gymnasium floor
is waxed like lips
is so slick you can see
your own reflection
and admire it
and, admiring it
wish it was enough.

THINGS ARE NOT AS BAD AS THEY SEEM

Confession: that there is in fact an end
to winter and its relentless reinvention,
sheath ice cracking from pines,
road signs visible again and asphalt warming,
the frozen beets in the root cellar
beginning their history of nurture and pickle and store.

The cats trail like wedding bands
behind the boys who sell what they call
spare blood in jars and their compelling
stories of salt and postage.
We spend recent evenings in complacence
and ambivalence, not worrying the season out
but enduring its remainder.

For $15, those blood-selling boys
will pester the last ice from the driveway with hoes
resulting in tool-ring and clatter,
the feverish grins on their faces
new with exertion.

I find a daisy petrified in barn light
when I undo the lock on the door.
Fresh tracks, a magnifying glass,
a sleeping bag that reminds me of a pupa,
and a worn copy of *Penthouse Forum*:
these remainders of human secrets.

Even the postcard from my posthumous mother reeks of Spring.

Prisoners in the county jail
sting the bars with cups and pens
and rings signaling release.

The new television station in town
broadcasts its first, brought to you
by Northwest Airlines and the few
living original members
of the Lawrence Welk orchestra.

Smoke signs from the cabins still brave the lake.

Deciduous trees restock.

The lake ice separates and slows out;
a few floes stagger like commas to the breakers.

Season is a decision.

What seams there are in the world
unstitch and shudder and fade.

SELF-PORTRAIT WITH TRANSGRESSION

Chain of being, chain around my ankle
that keeps me always tethered to the earth,
that keeps my awful long-gone emphysema uncle
underneath the crusty surface—no rebirth

no reincarnation, instant breakfast
surprising in a can, chemical and
stunningly delicious. This is the half-

way point, a spike, a peak, the weakest ham-
handed overture to Orpheus, his
customized & mirrored-window hearse adorned

with the biggest radio antenna
in the long white weather world—please return
with me, help me return her to her breath
which was bad, but better than the other.

LAWRENCE WELK DIES

And men in Craftmatic adjustable beds recline,
their hearts on momentary pause—my father
one of them; all our fathers one of them, those
fathers who made us turn the show on to light
up evenings otherwise irreducibly devoted
to the one long task, shoveling the snow back
from the driveway—six inches accumulation
each hour, and the plows steady on the roads,
plowmen grinning, filled with Citgo "Cappuccinos"
and old mail-order mints. Pine-smelling fathers
in from the woods and that hack day of work
felling Christmas trees with manual saws back
and forth and axe-arcs generated by shoulders,
let loose into air. That man in the great suit
and those twin conducting arms long enough
for two trombones is dead. And liquor is still
being sold to minors trolling in on snowmobiles—
machines that serve as proof of age—and men
are losing limbs. The old high school is down;
all that architecture dusted, and the future is on
skis cross-countrying towards this house tonight.
That future has a thirty-ought strapped to its back,
bolt-action digging in below the scapula and xyphoid
process. Kids in school are still afraid to perform
mouth-to-mouth on that nasty dummy, in spite
of all the antiseptic sprays and what-if-it-was-your-
dying-sisters? Who among us will be the one to press
our lips to it, to breathe that cord of wood
back to life, to take up the old and greased
garage sale trombone, lead the band, stun
a life right out of Branson and the Lennon
Sisters and listen to that Jo Ann Castle play.

OUTLINE TOWARDS AN ANTIDOTE: I

I. Dote for days
    a. on the image of the wreck
    b. on the still-ticking clock
       you nicked from the wreck
       while no one else had thought to look
       still shrunk in the plastic wrap
       now hanging naked on your wall
       a departure totem, common
       as a memory
    c. on your thoughts after passing
    d. on discussion questions asked
       at the book club a week
       after the lake effect snow
       that caused the wreck,
       a crack in the ticker-tape
       of space and time and stuff like that
              i. questions on Russell Banks'
                 The Sweet Hereafter—a sequence of specks
                 on a page when read in Braille,
                 a pattern of bulbs tucked into a garden
                 long under snow, now coming up,
                 a brickwork of stars that we decode
                 with fingertips, some training, hope
                 of rain for weeks to wash the dam away,
                 and fireworks to illuminate the sky
                 and whatever's left behind it.

OUTLINE TOWARDS AN ANTIDOTE: II

II. Then enough about the wreck
   a. its backbone worth of glass
   b. the sack of potatoes
      unintentionally mashed in the back—
      since stores were running out of stock,
      you thought you'd stash some away
      in preparation for what you hoped
      would be the last lash of winter weather,
      which in a way it was
   c. the scattered socks from the plastic bag
      soaked and molding through, the kind
      of nasty trophies a cat would steal and covet
   d. enough about the songs still playing
      on the radio until it shorted out
      and sputtered softly to a static halt
      (did it sound like ashes crackling after fire?)
   e. enough about the bucks that troll the roads
      and cause these accidents, enough about
      the rack, the felted skull brought home and mounted
      after the accident and the later mercy killing—
      a trophy of survival which, this time, you lack.

OUTLINE TOWARDS AN ANTIDOTE: III

III. Convince me that you're gone
a. that you're not just stunned
    in a gutter somewhere coasting out the storm
b. that you've not carried this joke much too far—
    your backpack that we filled with onions
    and bricks, a salt lick, some wood for fires, some
    beer, all making it so heavy you nearly snapped
    your back, you said, that we then unpacked
    and shared the load more reasonably among us
c. show me that you're not the ghost in the asphalt heart
    of Highway 41, body buried in the start loop up by
    Copper Harbor, before it winds down traitor south
d. if you're not gone or stunned but ghost
    then haunt me like a ghost

SYNONYM

After Liz, my X, my axe to break the freeze
that had settled on the body, after she
had passed the coroner's fly-and-acid tests
had made her way through customs, through the ice
to the other Canada (the one
requiring all the ink to gather, stain
its name on paper, so that the Rorschach
left was the only way to talk about it)

there was another X, a minor Liz
a stand-in twin—her own identical
fingerprinted same, who came with legs &
her very own heart murmur, who had lived
in true Canada (the one with curling
and the blots of hockey pucks scattered
after practice on the rink)

whom I only learned of in the last two days
before the surprise departure of the X
I loved but to whom I could not confess it.
Would this new she sit for me, gift me
with surplus kisses—those rinds, remainders
of the dreams I had—would the same
words I used for the old X
serve the new as well?

VACATIONLAND

This place, this bearer of the chilly winter burst,
the white-out everywhere and flurry,
the not-in-the-terms-of-Dairy-Queen,
this blizzard with a lowercase *b*,
far from commercial in its constancy,
its threat, impact, and our recovery:
always from it. We are always re-shoveling
out the driveways and panking down the snow
or breaking up the ice with handmade iron spears
or spokes wrested from bikes that have succumbed
at last to rust. This is my vacationland, my very own
Misery Bay, my dredge, my lighthouses, my vanishing
animal tracks in snow. Everyone who is not from here
is *not from here*, and that is all there is to say.
Everyone from here is still *from here*
regardless of where they are or where they end.

White light filtering through snow like dust.
There is always light coming down
like a donation from God— a little perk
to get us through the winter—upon us.
This light lights up our faces, lights up the faces
of the frozen dead as seen on TV from Canada.

This vacationland, this motel open year-round,
is now a Best Western and that is good, I guess.
This vacationland, this Michigan,
my Michigan, is no destination, no getaway
for us, those who are always *from.*
We have no destinations. We have no way
to get away from her, from here, to get away
from romantic winter getaways and those
who've come to get away from dull bombs of city lives.
We cannot get away from *from* and from the doldrum
winter silent burn. We might as well be stone—agates,
mottled trifles, appearing periodically on the beach

to be taken home, to be put with other pretty rocks
and bits of lake glass in jars. We are meant for your mantel
and for the light that will find us there.

We might as well be the kind of rock
that passes for rock on the radio up here,
meaning Foreigner and Journey and nothing
that could be ever meaningful again
because it has been subsumed by soft-rock
crap-rock, classic-rock, by radio, by frequency-
modulated energy in air, by the tyranny
of awful playlists and shitty DJs
and no hope of getting a decent song
played for us to be indifferent to at prom.

We are what is left. We are drift.
I guess this is a sort of manifesto.

ANSWERS TO EXAMINATION QUESTIONS

(1) yes (2) the colossus (3) a bloodless cross-ice pass
(4) apex & crux (5) late night shift with fear of hold-up
(6) one-fourth (7) feel loved, regardless of what your
father says (8) related to your difficulties with girls (9)
pine resin on wood (10) "Take me home tonight"
(11) bits of graduation speech, overblown & soporific
(12) *spragmos*, from the Greek, "to tear limb from limb,
dismember" (13) file finish (14) star in cast iron (15) to
leave (16) suggestion of lemon pledge scent
(17) dismantle (18) your brother's breath moored in
freezing air (19) an unstoppable plan (20) true necessity
of prom (21) light & weight (22) to go without
(23) discarded code (24) the purpose of the witness
(25) cancelled check & locker key (26) both a & c
(27) permission to reprint your love letters in all detail
(28) stunned conundrum (29) esophagus & throat (30)
b., before you knew (31) no (32) cored (33) to show
the interior construction of an object (34) sink risk &
rink (35) triage (36) brief love action (37) 3/8 (38)
punctuated by silence (39) at your locker after your
death, feeling returnable & empty (40) answers come by
dream or autopsy (41) formal considerations (42)
paregoric (43) how blood moves when stirred up
(44) to excise (45) over, now, done (46) parabolic arc
(47) pilot light, out (48) bitter bullet anger strong enough
to keep you up at night (49) sound or explanation
(50) somnambulist (51) Pastor Sam's sinister daughter
(52) dot-dot-dot, dash-dash-dash, dot-dot-dot
(53) delinquency & bell-ring (54) "its" instead of "it's"
(55) instance of violent crime (56) everybody drowns
or is consumed (57) voice & face (58) sour & spur
weather (59) the remembered life.

THREE

Maybe there
is a way
beyond the
winter and
the weather:
less directed
elegies and
love poems

VESSEL

One way to get beneath it all
to access desire again
is to reawaken pain—
this is what leads me to black
the skin on my left hand
on too-hot iron. I never claimed
that the bright moon
constantly above us
(with its steady drift of wax and wane)
was mine.

Char, dead
nerve stemming like a tulip
through the epidermis,
awake again like a father on a holiday,
breakfast tray laid like a sash
across your chest while we wait
along the sides of the white room.

I desire
your bloom and anagram again,
that motion, action, dissolution.

INVENTORY ELEGY 3:
The Dirty Entry

- Polaroid of you undressed
- pervasive nail polish scent
- impact auto safety glass
- your lack of balance
- evidence of cloth and hearing
- persuasion
- salt-lick neck hair
- ropes and cordage, debris on
- flame-lick stop sign light
- your first Halloween without dry ice witch punch
- Ford Fairmont vinyl seat
- cake meant for you to pick up: bundt
- eyeglass frame: rubber, wire
- repeated calls for you at home; my anger

PROPOSED SELF-ELEGY WITH TORQUE

The flowers were what I most looked forward to:
poinsettias like hymns in pots and lilies
for the potluck table-setting—such well-lit
& dull clichés, they go without mention
like metal goes for long without lick
or polish—but they were true, resplendent
and the whole shebang went off without a hitch.

Your Uncle Paul did not have to be cued
to finish his Polack jokes. Every eulogy was just
sincere enough. The organist slow-mo-ed at the keys,
the pedals humping up and down like boys
in pins and ties and church-starched white shirts
like the just-interred and quite-surprised dead

dreaming of whale-hump then blow
and sound, and great pyramid apex
and Cinemax late-night
like they were at sea and sick
without remotes, and nothing else was on.

Then everyone left
for the after-party narration
and the coin-op beds
that vibrate in the Budget Inn.

Everyone had scurvy,
ate lemons,
then got better.

Burial is like this.

The sun was clean;
the dirt was soft enough;
the brandless cigarettes, half-off
at the reservation Citgo down in Baraga.

The wind was more than usual.
Fire Danger: Moderate.
Boats on the lake.
In Canada it was Boxing Day.

You who gather wire & Ziploc bags
saltpeter & your mother's torn-up skirts
Vaseline & cannon fuse
to make plastique,

You who diversify your BB gun portfolio
as you grow older and take more serious aim
with a ten-pump w/scope at passing-by
rear station wagon windows,

You who drink the homemade
150-proof *sadiki* we bought and smuggled
in from Cyprus to impress you,

By the time you get this paradox,
you'll be the rumor of gas & glass
cigarette light between lips
Atomic Fireball residue in a mouth or smeared on paper
an assignment half-completed like a will, unclear
an answer key with ink in every circle:
no ABACAB, ABC, or BAD DAD
but a mass of black a calendar of crows
a conglomeration
a messy epitaph
a shotgun pattern gloss of ink
that could have been arm-meant
or suggestive of adolescent love on walls.

MOVING THROUGH ETHER

Things we learn after you had gone:
your greasy fingers under Sheryl's blouse beneath
the collapsible bleachers, recorded on undeveloped film,
lists of names on lined paper for unknown reasons,
bags of things we had thought gone into air
or gnome-stolen, $2 bills tucked like glossy
magazines underneath the bed.

This is a pornography, what we do
to understand the dead.
We splay you out on the family
room table where your sisters
gather your possessions, hold them
to their chests—they are slow dancing
through ether. This ritual is invite-only,
and though we knew it should be private,
we knew when asked we would attend.

It is a coming out, unintentional, full
of tension, mass and mess. We sort, sift,
sieve, and divvy—Harriet gets the AAA
ashtray, smoky glass that says *God Is From Indiana!*
(surely this must be true) because she is
a smoker with troubled lungs and lipstick lips;
and I will take the set of typing books
stolen from the old high school
before it was reassigned to dust: *College
Typewriting with Personal Problems*,
3rd Edition, by D.D. Lessenberry.

I remember you in homeroom,
your fingers arched on home row
in that class, *a-s-d-f*, herons dipping into the black
of *j-k-l-;*—that mass of click and ink and register.

Mrs. Liitanen who taught the course,
who would sob halfway through word recognition drills,
who could never time us right on words-per-minute,
who pitched an IBM Selectric through the glass
of a third-floor window to the asphalt below,
who was one week later hit by a Bluebird
school bus just outside the school,
who was henceforth the subject
of an amateurish documentary,

and whom we remember like most things
that we still remember—halfway, not fondly,
nor do we count ourselves lucky
to have witnessed her Halloween wings and wigs,
but as an experience that we got through,
like consecutive Christmases sans family,
like we got through everything like drifts
of snow or booze or long division until now.

SNOW AMNESIA

It's like Jesse was never here at all, he's been so long
gone, like a gunshot that leaves no print—
no motive, modus operandi, no finger-trace behind, no black.
So many through the crust via snowmobile

or car, and you behind, hulking like a buoy,
unwilling like a battery, left out in all
kinds of weather. The neon sign on the Vacationland
motel is like an epitaph through snow:

"NO VACA" is all it says tonight, its molecules
stirred up, bright like an orange rind
would be if those things burned or could be lit
or strung up like lines of K-Mart lights

and left to dangle after the holidays
and all the tourists have come and gone and gone.

♣

All the town has come and come and gone
to and from the funeral home which, like a holiday,

is rife with lights
(is it so important that the dead be this well-lit?)
and potluck gifts for both the teary and the stoic. The gravy's rind
is setting as we speak, like how ice resets itself, its molecules

dancing (like in *Fantasia*), magic, back to whole. The snow
comes down like grace, and we forget. This is no vacationland
for me and mine. Pick any family out of all
the phone book Finnish names: that blood has lost a boy

or father to the weather, on foot or on a snowmobile.
This night's snow, your brand-new grave. Your ash is black
against it until shoveler or storm. Your name imprinted
on or in it, only for so long.

SONNET: NOTES FROM X WHICH MIGHT TURN OUT
TO BE AN ELEGY, STEMMING FROM THE U.S. MAIL

A postcard from the X, emblem of death
or dollar signs like candlelight in eyes,
the crux and crucifix, the map the mark,
the ink drop spot, the patch stitched in the crotch
that holds your snowmobile suit together,
objective of your love, known otherwise
as architecture, made of point and arc
and light, still life of glass and ice and crust,

math bartered in the margins of your text,
the liquor fix, the hex, the pox, the axe
accident resulting in my brother,
axle greased as slick as 6, surrender
at Appomattox, and the apex from
which everything is down is else is done.

WHAT IS LESS THAN FIRE IS LESS THAN X

The B&B bar burns down and you eat flames
in your windshield, wend your way to work through
man-high drifts fat with buried drunks. Your un-
successful neighbor tries suicide with
a shotgun, glowers through half a face en
route to the emergency room where he
will wait a half hour of groan and inter-
com for his uncle to arrive.

Incised flesh is one answer to a wait
as handheld beam is one solution to
a gone-sour date and long home plod, no kiss.
The metal bone that's in your shin sings ray-
ray-radio: bad Top Forty songs from
1985 when you rode the yell-
filled yellow bullet bus to school, and your
hands were made of fists.

Knowing lack of understanding early
grief, your third grade teacher left for cancer
and did not return. Knowing only slow
song repair for old love and construction
of the most elaborate paper snow-
flakes. The skill of sieve and lace and never
getting over anything is what you
learned that year. Knowing remembrance

and remonstrance, Christian tracts found at St.
Vincent de Paul and used for your papier-
mâché reconstructions of remembered
breasts. Knowing prosthetic, mathematic,
that your arm is apparatus, made of
diagram, some luck, and force. Requiring
maintenance instead of sustenance, so
it says in the witty printed manual.

Your uncle trades his antique guns in for
time and what we hope is good talk with his
wife between here and Chicago to pre-
vent that end. Riots on TV tonight
and the broadcast close to a drawn and drawn-
out war. What comes through the telephone line
is garble, fury, full of sound and wine
that is algebra to you.

ELEGY FOR THE END OF MINES AND FUNCTION

Laura says a lung sings coal
and some men are trapped for weeks in dark
guts of mines with forty-five degree
slanted shafts, canaries sunk in metal casks,
the remaining parts of light
that ease down from the world above.

The work of rock
is shift and chip and fault.
Time is air defined by wax
and drip and ease, some old chum slump,
the widening of crack, the sudden dark begin,
air pressure punctuated by blast
and drop, the long-persisting sorrow echo.

A rush of air brings scent to the casket—
a dish to the potluck
a hostess gift that glistens, is tasteful,
will look good on the mantel
with the candlesticks and sporty pictures of the boys.

Now those pictured boys infiltrate the closed-down mines,
come equipped with tins of aerosol,
cigarettes, and glossy magazines. Aluminum and glass,
propane gas grills and coolers
stacked with meat. This is process, black-box
flow-chart understanding,
madness, method, necessary rite.

It is written on the walls
that you must clip the lock
to go below, or cut the chain-mesh
fence, bring at least a meal with you,
follow lode like your father,
learn what you can of ore.
Anything that cannot be grown
must be forged or minted,
must be mined or meant.

THE BLOOD, THINKING

of cellophane and Mason jars, vacuumed shut,
Contact paper sheer, holding dry deflowered
flies and weevils tight against the page. Stems
and blossoms pressing liquid out, the dead
humping in the ground in which the rhubarb—
vein-like—flowers and cuts root. Where
has the griefkeep gone? Where is the bloodjar
kept? In which salt cellar, roosting under whose
pickled beets, brown, reclusing, getting into dance—
how the boards jump above, and the hi-hat
bounds up like a dog or eager heart.

The blood thinking of spin
jumps rope and kicks in its can and dreams of being
spilt across Formica tables or Michigan McDonalds'
faux-copper tart tops complete with creeks,
pits, and seniors' names strip-mined into them
with pocket knives and pens:
the waterways through which it might course
and learn another language.

Ah! the blood dreaming of love
like karate or bald eagle-style kung fu
knows it's a ninja moves like a ninja
has seen many movies and thinks
like a ninja caught in the shell of the lotus
throat full of its nectar, mouthing sweet words
at its awful proboscis the pistil
forgetting love's end then the grind
of the mortar and pestle.

The blood thinking of its only aspiration: vampire films
the cut across the throat, the questionable special effect
the collage of violins and shifting light
across the shot the décolletage—a rivulet
a bead, a road trip home or across the border of a country

moving down a collarbone, finding the meter
of the flesh, the friction coefficient
how the grades of highways limit
speed, how silent movies draw it out
how blood in black and white
is redder than the palm of any man just
come from splitting wood, the skin chapped rust
which means work dark against snow.

THE BLOOD PROPOSES THAT,
COME SPRING, WE MEET ON THE LAWN

The blood wants to matter, be relevant
again, celebrated like an event:
the running of the blood in spring
like the groaning cattle in Pamplona.

But for now it is the inner life,
the kick and toll that is what winter means:
quiet and in bursts, pressure-measured,
systole and diastole, sum of pour
and capillary, the hollow echo of a twin
blood-dead from birth, secreted
like a family secret or a precious stone.

The blood is thrilled on coffee
and strolls around the grounds
in search of summer love
or at least a dream approximation.

Its smear on a slide,
a sauce under the lens,
spread hors d'oeuvre-thin.

Being in love with the blood
means never having to spell hors d'oeuvre,
those clothespins loose and tinkling in the dryer
with the change from tolls and matted Kleenex bits
the memorized table-settings, rules
of punctuation, the true names of the dead.

Means acquiescence and atrophy, catastrophe.
Means water-ballerinas, clocks and limbs
synchronized to atomic time,
beamed straight to us from the coliseum.

Means remember and forget, otherness
and brother. Means center and encumbrance,
umber art on wall, circular cawing saw
and metal welder arc.

The blood will never bring lilies to the dinner
that you've—post-mortem—made.

Its thinness is its weakness, lack
of instinct for the clot, the scab,
that formalizes healing atop the cut,
foments interior, the repairing sulk.

This blood is bad. You've got to keep it in
like a tongue or like a sea
forever surging behind a dike.

THE BLOOD SAYS STUN

Stun it right out of the woods, the water
in the picture in the only picture
most vacationers have of the Northern
ear of Michigan, the land, the body

afloat in the water, the fists of lakes,
the blood says, yes, and stun all the tourists
with weather, with snow hanging under lamps

in stop-time unless kids have shot the lamps
out with no malice, all the stunned tourists
perched in the bar haze amid billiards, lakes

of light on the felt; the blood felt the body
like rosary beads once: something Northern
to clutch and worry—a daughter's picture
taken in woods, bone winter, in water.

EXCISION II

Found: one tiny eye
a lump, a deadened twin
a body in the body
size of a swirled cat's-eye
marble, beating snow- or heart-
globe just above the bicep.

Think this cyst a son
a giving birth
from the muscle's mouth
addition not subtraction
C-section carved
in the throwing arm
a Mariana trench
that holds the heavy water
and the bauble
that is cantilevered out
and tucked away in plastic
for a battery of tests.

Think this gauzy scrim
fit around the limb
a scaffolding or tie
a tourniquet
a charm around the arm
to keep the future out

and the left-behind line
a drooping pip-pip EKG
or epitaph, emblem, hem,
dumb balm, shorthand
for swerve or final passing
into snow country
where everything comes down,
quiet and all the time.

WHO ARE THE DEAD

and why number them or mark their graves
with newspapers or plastic flowers that will not wilt,
and why speak of them at all
since they will not return our calls,
come back, predict the punch lines of our jokes,
or troll our shores?

I am told I should be haunted by snowmobilers
clad in masks and leather letter jackets, kept up nights
by that awful shovel scrape when it hits concrete,
the *ding!* then spark of hoes breaking up the driveway ice.

Is that a fire or car alarm? Will the water level rise
above the dikes this year? Will it crest over every sandbag
that can be placed to keep that stream in check?
Will our mothers come back from Florida like they say,
or have they followed their hearts to other countries
where they don't have daylight savings time?

What's left: a litter of letters pouring through the door:
sympathies, recipes, dollar bills. Pictures of eyes and hand-
written notes promising to shovel our walk this winter for free
in light of our loss.

We are EZ-bake. Surveyors sighting roads
out through our scopes. We are plowmen clearing
town arteries; dumb plumbers dazed at leaking
water mains; interns standing in for surgeons
during short procedures. We are hypodermic,
biologic waste. We are biopsies wrapped in plastic
sacks and discarded. Are poets, executed for our poor taste
in clothes, or for ideals, or for other reasons.
We architects of country. Living wills,
last best testaments to grace. Listen,
glisten, you must find your way to light.

IMPLIED LOVE POEM

Tine, affix
yourself to vein:
let pewter spine
of light-caught, lentil-spear
collectible utensil
complete its jab and hanker
for my fragrant wrist.

Your wish for immersion
in the bone, and tilling of the skin
fairy-granted, bruise-blue and true
since all is hole and graft and fail.

Since my love, my errant burr,
my deft and arctic tern,
my reverberating Iowa,
my plain, my pop-up girl,
is gone and off and dead,
caught like a ball, aloft
just before the final buzzer

circling like a bird for wire,
a nasty black and addled grackle,
all cylinders afire for roost
on any electric line.

How elegant they are,
aggregates of feather and utility,
prooflike and stream-thin,
made for the swoop and milky
crap, that loose bomb,
that car glass splat.

Terse and tensile buzzard,
how do you perch prehensile
with all the fiber optics
(the land's Ziploc bag and freezer burn)
humming just below
(or are those cords buried, and those above
just antiquated, old
like past-date soup,
like cans and string)?

How can you chirp
and hack and mock
while I wind and moan
below, gnash enamel
down to gum

and proceed to shit
in the designated spot,
the whitest life
of toilets
that appear to me
perhaps overly
bleach-loved,
disinfected,
tended to,

when all information is an omen,
every bulletin, a bone
a hull a bullet.

THERE ARE THINGS I NEED TO TELL YOU ABOUT BREATH

For starters, that your dragon steam release in winter air
remedies nothing like it does the cold

while we stand under lamps with metal necks
transfixed by all the hanging snow

that is the threat of radio and infrared
and mutual assured destruction shown as false

in the nth rebroadcast of *Red Dawn* on TBS.
If shook like foil or artificial in a ball,

we could name this motion thunder
and say what we liked best about sudden light

this time of year. Morning has you up
from your dream of frozen iron, meat,

and economics. If you still have the electric knife
from your father's last and final marriage,

then this is love and plausible.
If it's sold, garaged, returned to Sears,

then all art is accident, all birds stuffed above
the mantel not time-stop but taxidermy,

and all gasoline on soil is simply spill
not pigment, delta, or corona.

SNOW MERIDIAN

With a butter knife, you, my love, divide your throat in two
along the white tissue line that means we are above
the snow meridian and its predictions of unending winter
peace. Everything tonight is trace—dead light from stars

through leaves' remains twinkling on the limbs,
evidence of tinsel in the rug, breath-cloud thunderhead,
wadded ATM receipts discarded after the transaction,
residual warmth of seats in the airport departure lounge,

the trails of international jet liners taking off above us
and the meaning of those lights / that roar: we go bright
and deaf for the next minute and sometimes slick
tips of ice leaven our faces like maple keys in Fall.

This reminds the season in us and we feel old
just this once, we keep our balance on the Ford
Fairmont's hood that holds the creases that catalog
all the takeoffs and our bodies here. What is a scar

on a face but shorthand for wall or axe or auto accident.
What is stitch but ants' jaws approximation, a fault a saying yes
a line on the body, an avid affirmation of the skin's
will to close, keep in its heat and great divide.

WHAT IF THERE IS NO ICE

What if there is no ice
no Jesse, no Liz, no X, no equal sign
no skin on the lake to offer us answers
no long gone winter song
no throng of mourners
black in coats against the white
dikes that line the sides of roads
when plows have passed—

What if there is no lake at all
no wet mouth on stampsand
(the iron ore afterbirth)
no hive for fish no base to rap against
with your head while diving
no repository for your bones
no grief node—

What if there is no snow
no sign of weather left behind
on rinks or on the hill behind Pamida
that kids sled down & hope
they can stop before entering the highway—

What if there is no mine no earth
to tunnel through, no father disappearing
into the ground each day—what if all is gas
is blocks of shattered glass beautiful on the floor,
or tests in school: all transparency and hard
to hold, easy to be wrong about,
easy to inhale or burn, go through.

I HAVE A THEORY ABOUT THIS ELEGY

Because I mean ash when it snows shushs and esses
from the factory, because the heifers tottering
in the field in ice coats moan low, because the half
of the family that believes in love is bleeding internally
and that is sad and a secret way of thinking,
because Hilarious Harry, the lone elephant in the circus
that came through town last week and escaped and roamed
the roads froze eventually, because diamonds
are just another form of fuel and airplanes streaming
engine smoke barely make it this far north to land
on the strip, because any event comes packaged
with a frozen reason, because this season is a bone
that will not end not ever not in harm or myth,
will not end in fever under blankets under wool,
will not end with winter sin out behind the outhouse
that—too—is frozen through, all the shit like copper
veining in the ground, because everything is slow
as it gets this time of year without dying (or in some cases
dying anyway), because this winter is the worst
and can be quantified as such by snowmobiling deaths
per day, per month, and winter inches
judged along a graduated pipe, and trauma etiologies,
because your mother's will was never publicly read
at any volume and your marriage was never interrupted
by a woman screaming before Speak Now and Forever Hold
Your Peace, and besides I was too self-involved
to send a card or note or care, apparently,
because your wedding was a chamois cloth
or tongue along a fender, because your mother
was just another one of all the preening dead
that year that queued postmortem at the bank
that is the mausoleum waiting for the winter
freeze, all skull and lonely quotient,
there is no clause or mention that can balance
this sentence and end this equation, solve
for X in moonlight and radio, or make up
for anything ever, which is sad & such & so & on.

BIG FUNGUS ELEGY FOR X AS METEOR

Listen, list, my meteor, X
skylight & bright face of rock
hook and penitent line horizoning
over the top of winter weather systems
where WHUH tops out in ionosphere
and slivers into half Hank Williams
half textbook $a < n$, half what my terminal
grandmother termed *what have you*
in her last pre-departure algebra,

Deliver me a post-Christmas blast
an FTD flaming pick-me-up bouquet
astronomical and expensive as a funeral
or build-your-own telescope, or tourniquet,

Apply your awful cosmic balm
to this skin thin as $=$
or the tiny operations of division
that happen all the time,

Rub it in to me and rub me out
my sci-fi Christ, my matchstick man gone burn
with fright and amputation, my father-made
my greater-than, my anvil, snap-on tool
my doe and antidote,

Drive me shotgun like a graph
or mafia out to the lichen mass,
the Upper Mich. humongous fungus,
largest single life in the hemisphere,
equation remnant and final evidence
of proof or last big-ass design,

Finalize my life as light on screen
show your work, chiaroscuro
set me compass path and coping saw
make me lather, lathe, woodburning kit
soldering iron and solid precipitated out

of my cliché genetic twist
cut me ink on stone
or stone on flesh
raise me exponential, trigonomic
(spell-checker says "tragicomic? ergonomic?"),

Save me like a secret note
and yes my unknown X
you function, nothingness
you absence absolute,
black box headlock of a girl
if this is not a love poem, nothing is
and so on, Q.E.D..

POST-MORTEM PARTY TRICK

Dear Dead Jesse,
appreciate the postcard,
coming as it did well after
the funeral meats had been cleared
away and all the streamers, poor
and limp and black, had been filed
permanently under trash.

It driftwooded in the mail
like your thin and flimsy ghost:
obligatory flamingos,
necks transmuted into hula
hoops or smoke rings caught
in glass, hand-cancelled in Florida
which is more Polaroid than state.

It shames my fridge collection
and that straight bullshit flush
with which you won my old Pontiac
no thanks to Jacob M. and his quick
card-stack hands. This, though, magic
of another order—like the thefts
you would perform during open lunch
in high school at the Freedom
gas station, only better—such grand delinquency,
such fine results: crappy eighties rock tapes,
cigarettes and Jolly Ranchers, liquor fifths
all kangarooed on your slim frame

which now lies in the mausoleum
with all the other doubters
and your loot
which will be interred
when the ground is warm enough to dig
barring some new sleight
of hand or weather, which I cannot
make myself believe
is beyond you.

A BRIEF ELEGY FOR TEETH

And specifics—enamel hard like brick-
layers' arms but not so sun-toned,
not browned by serious work
so much as stained by love's slow departure
and that unrelenting night-grind and wake-
up ache. It's hard to give up winter,
living South because of you,
discard the drive through drifts
high like dikes or dirty moats, and sleds
bulleting through backstops into traffic.

Hard to tap the artery of staying-in-
because-of-cold, get back to where you,
alcoholic, are, idea-full and laying up
your glass on any varnished bar.

Our English teacher Mr. Woodruff
who had his own word in the dictionary
would show up to class some days glistening
with liquor-ease and sweat,
listening for any sign of moan
or complaint from any one of us,
ready to hold forth at any time on epiphany
and Joyce. He lost his fingers,
toes from prolonged exposure and a sense-
less honor act, winter camping in the Smoky Mountains.
He had teeth brittle like glass or Chiclets.
Did I mention the dictionary word?

He'd never tell us which—*greyhound,
griddle cake, gridiron, plainclothes, plainer,
plainsman, plainsong.* Walleyed, unrelenting,
he'd eschew cars and instead bike drunk
to pubs and back, using words as bombs
like *unrelenting* and *eschew.*

Lover, I regret any act
that took me from you,
separated arm from shoulder,
ligament from bone. Now scour
Webster for solution: *threnody,*
some consolation, *dirge.*

ELEGY FOR THE END OF WEATHER

After the moon has cleared the earth's edge
and has ceased to be surprising in the sky,
the remaining winter birds have dropped
from flight to roost on fence-posts and you
and I are still together in your car on our backs
in a ditch with the interior light flicking on
and off. Your breath comes out fast
when you let it, and it fogs the glass
with its weight. Snow has stopped its nightly
accumulation song. We are far from home,
in Minnesota without AAA or phone.
Headlights dim. I fingernail our names
into the frost: *A loves M.* So there. I exhume
a laugh from you. This is a crisis of eyelids, headlights,
steam in air, and hair still wet from sweat or shower
now stiffened up in cold. Icarus is tied up
in the trunk with only Pepperidge Farm Goldfish for food
and your parents will soon begin their wonder
and call-around. No traffic for a half-hour now.
I count imaginary cars on my imaginary hand.
Your father who is an economist
and who describes snow as debt, and love
as capital gains will not find us slid
under a bank of snow and several
meaningful inches. Imagine the world
like this always—slow and cold and static.
Think sky and paper plate
moon as I move it across the roof.
Think this cigarette ash fine white Florida sand
and the leopard-print lighter a flare, a fire.
Think Icarus our savior if we could get out
to let him out. Free him from twine
and let him try the sky for help.

VACATIONLAND

What does doing it accomplish, this morning's
mourning over steam caused by the exposure
of the coffee to the air—
                              its coils and licks
reminiscent of a spring with constant k
which measures how much compression it can take
before failing—
                    this note a sort of temporary cliché
we call the elegy designed to celebrate
and confirm our loss, reduce our big grief sum,
this ore we have worked from the lode, from the loam,
with our hands, this ore we lug from year
to year with our ears always shame-aflame or filled
with itch from our names just crossing people's lips?

I keep my tiny store of grief beneath all the salt:
in the shaker, in the cellar, clapped within a cozy,
away from air which might reduce it
or sun which might convert it to what
I won't recognize and can no longer use.

Sometimes I bring it out like a declaration.
I knead it and return it to the dark.

Can it take me away from here, from infinite precipitation
and blizzard mound, from center of whatever
storm constantly surrounds us?

Can it get me to the coast—
                              to any coast—
to any place from which I can overlook the sea
and get beyond myself for good?

I would close it off as I do the basement during flood.

I would burn it away like the night's leftovers
on the grass in morning, reminders of the evening
like drunken Post-It notes or drink rings
left through lack of constant coaster action
on all the wood throughout the house.

Have I come to depend upon it, on my rigid grip on it
like a blankie, like a bottle—
                              I should go to AA
(or maybe AAA) to see what God can do for me today.

To Whom It May Concern,
I'd like to file my third complaint
against the world.

SELF-PORTRAIT W/BACKPACK
THAT IS FILLED WITH ONIONS
AND THAT MAY BE EMBLEMATIC OF X

The carry—not the packing—
is the trick. Not the nose-hold
and eye-well and piling-up
the rucksack with onions
whose sharpness is proportional
to age. But to mount
the bag on bony shoulder
regardless of its future
uselessness or difficult lift.

To hold the burden like
a burden must be held
through any worthwhile
dream, when clarity is glossy
and slips away like canola oil
zipped in bags and sweating
through, the wet hand drool
no recompense for college
try for A for effort.

Do not gaze up at the night,
at its crappy stars, tiny wrecks
still covered in post-crash glass.

Do not let the pot go low
oiled with ghee, goose grease,
and boiling on the stove.

This is answer, an embalming
of the body. This soup, fiasco,
made of cut and solo moan.

This recipe cannot not be borne
or passed down like baseball
skills or secrets of disease
but must be found and built
from scratch each time.

ELEGY FOR THE ODD,
WHERE IT DRAINS,
WHERE IT ENDS

This blood is odd and good
and comes from what is dead:

necks hacked or sawed-off into buckets
that we keep in the shed

for this last task before all
the animals are done for the Fall

and the rest of the year.
Sometimes we drain the chickens' blood

into the wild dill
that grows behind the fence.

Does that blood follow veins
in the ground all the way

to the root? Does it drain
into groundwater? Why can't we taste

it—there's so much we haul
off to the soil and out into the aqueduct

our fathers made behind the shed
to carry all the blood away

that we don't give to the dill.
Otherwise the raccoons get it,

eyes lit and glittering
in the evening, raucous Sinatras

among the cans we try to bungee closed.
I put a tiny daisy bud

in a test tube, send it down the trough
which we never followed long enough

to find out where it ends,
where our fathers' hands have made

it end—in sewer grates,
or illegally into the streets

in the middles of nights
where kids see it drain

and think *murder, possibility,*
guilt, and *sin,* and sing.

SOME OF THE BONE HAS GONE MISSING

That chip, that snippet from a song
indicator of the body's strength
that we kept in the jar used for killing
butterflies when we were strong and young

is gone. The blood—long singing
in the other jar, long dreaming
of logs in churning river water, long
going downstream in felled-pine

dreams of springs and melting snow
rushes, smelt, and log-stunned rainbow
trout wheeling aimless in the stream—
remains aloft, a thought, a doffed

cap reverie in the now-still pool
of dust & light, remains alone, sans bone.

MIAMI

End's end, and now the elegy is gone
deserted like a bumper sticker on
the Aerostar you sold last year, or
a winter carnival tent, the ice sculptures

releasing, slimming, slumming down to just
above a hum, that freezing point (which is not
fixed like science or the rules for overcoming grief
but spread out on the roads like salt).

You can pass through this like weather
like a turnstile like a sausage maker.
This is some light. The other side.

This is an elegy for elegies. Ask the amputees
about their lives beyond the accidents,
about their limbs that still—electric—twitch.

GRANDIOSE ELEGY FOR D = RT

Liz your party is a wreck
all the streamers down like birds
dead & face-first on the snow-encrusted lawn
and I am apologizing for this
like an architect would
for his skewed erection of a building
seeing what it—when built—obscured.

Both of us have been circumspect
about the objects of our obsessions:
so for the record, for the eulogy
I'm sure I won't be asked to make,
mine is (for the most part): you
—you symbolized by weather
and by letters on the page.

Yours, I know: velocity,
the achievement of distance over time
—the story of impact and submission,
your teeth embraced by wire
—the promises of violence towards glass
—hair's wet and perpendicular reward
frozen straight out from your scalp

like light in lines in movies
like how icicles might grow
except for gravity's sad-sack fact.

I will take all the distance that I can get from this event.
I will gorge myself on all of the reception food and take some home.
I will comb the stories in the paper and learn them like a catechism.

I will not say your name for a week, then longer.
I will encrypt this story in symbol and secret
—logic and longing and telephone static.

I will dial this long-distance dedication in
to Casey Kasem, or Rick Dees, or whoever is leftover
droning out the weekly top four-oh on WHUH,
the station that you always railed against
(and I'm sure the radios that overlook
whatever platform you wait on
for whatever late-arriving train
will carry it and blare it out full-blast)

and that will make a difference
and that will prove my point
which I think is about how light works
along the scapula and clavicle

—is about white on black or the reverse
—is snowshoe or cross-country ski
—is weight distributed across a surface, equally

—is making its way through snow
like a dog to home
—is $sin(X)$ and $cos(Y)$
—is your inscription in my book on trigonometry

—is after all of this like the end of weather
which is known as Spring
with its once-again addition
(a small sedition, a brief mercurial climb)
which feels like emigration
or the reinstatement
of the temporary privileges of the heart.

AERIALIST

It is easy only now to tell you this.
That being gone is like from a fissure
yelling back to sky. That this construction
yellow tape is all I have left over.

That this girder—on which I sit and hoot
like a loon a hundred feet above
the street—is my only chair. That the stone
lions propped on top of the D&N

building are here for me alone (among
the dead only I crave heights), and for the few
important hearts delivered by chopper to the pad.

What I thought I had was dust and shiny
string looted thereafter by birds, amen. Now I
am alone and aerial, all afterbirth and light.

DEBTS AND THANKS

There are many friends to whom I owe various debts. This is a short attempt to address some of these: Mike Baran, Leonard Blackburn, Josh Borgmann, Robin Brooks, Jen Bunyar, Mike Dombrowski, Shannon Fields, Matt Frederickson, Lauren Goodwin, Heidi Gotz, Paul Guest, Alicia Holmes, Mary Ann Hudson, Kris Ingmundson, Sophia Kartsonis, Emma Ramey, Christopher Roman, Andy Segedi, Abraham Smith, Neil Smith, Sarah Squire, Alison Stine, Matt Vadnais, Eliot Khalil Wilson, Nicole Willey, and Rob Young.

I owe a lot, too, to teachers, past and present: Neal Bowers, Joel Brouwer, Randy Freisinger, Sandy Huss, Deb Marquart, Sheryl St. Germain, and Bruce Smith.

Thanks to Jeffrey Levine and Tupelo for taking this thing on.

To my family, certainly—both here and gone.

And to Megan, for all that is necessary.

NOTES, WHEN NECESSARY, ON THE POEMS

"Vacationland": The Vacationland Motel is outside of Houghton, Michigan, on the way to Chassell, along U.S. 41 (about 45 miles from its beginning in Copper Harbor). Additionally, one of the ferries my grandfather piloted across the Straits of Mackinac was called the *Vacationland*

"After You've Gone On and Through": thanks to John Hazard for "opine"

"Approximation" is for Robert Young

"Outline Towards an Antidote: I": really, I'm talking about the Atom Egoyan version of *The Sweet Hereafter*, not the Russell Banks book

"Elegy for the End of Mines and Function": the line "a lung sings coal" is taken from a poem by Laura Didyk.

"Excision II": the last line is a remembered approximation of a Simon Perchik line.

"A Brief Elegy for Teeth" is for James Woodruff.

"Proposed Self-Elegy with Torque" includes a line lifted (not exactly) from Michael Sowder.

"Elegy for the End of Weather" is for Megan Campbell.

"Some of the Bone Has Gone Missing": the title is a Denise Levertov line.

"Miami": actually, I drove an Aerostar

"Grandiose Elegy for $D = RT$": for those who ditched too many high school physics classes, distance is equal to rate multiplied by time.

ACKNOWLEDGMENTS

Thanks to the magazines that originally published these poems
(sometimes in substantially different forms):

Another Chicago Magazine: "Alibi," "Grandiose Elegy for D = RT"
Ascent: "Elegy for the End of Weather"
Barrow Street: "from Contingency Elegy"
Blue Mesa Review: "Some of the Bone Has Gone Missing"
Chelsea: "Excision II," "I Have a Theory about this Elegy," "The Blood Proposes
    That, Come Spring, We Meet on the Lawn"
Conduit: "Index: A"
Drunken Boat: "Inventory Elegy 2," "There Are Things I Need To Tell You About
    Breath"
Ducky: "Vessel"
Faultline: "Things Come Up"
Fence: "Elegy Analogy I"
The Fiddlehead: "Proprietary Elegy"
FIELD: "Astonish"
Flyway: "Outline towards an Antidote: III," "Self-Portrait w/Backpack That Is Filled
    with Onions and That May Be Emblematic of X," "The Blood, Thinking"
Good Foot: "Elegy for the End of Mines and Function"
Grand Valley Review: "Things Are Not As Bad As They Seem"
The Greensboro Review: "After You've Gone On and Through"
Gulf Coast: "The Blood Says Stun," "Big Fungus Elegy for X as Meteor," "Snow
    Amnesia"
Indiana Review: "Outline Towards an Antidote: II"
The Journal: "Proposed Self-Elegy with Torque," "Who Are the Dead"
The Kenyon Review: "Elegy for the Odd, Where It Drains, Where It Ends,"
    "Konundrum Literary Engine," "Entry-Level Elegy," "Miami," "My Grandfather's
    Thumb"
Knock: "Inventory Elegy 3," "What Is Less Than Fire Is Less Than X"
I IT: "Answers to Examination Questions," "Summer Is a Mystery in Michigan" (as
    "Michigan Summer I"), "What If There Is No Ice,"
Mot Juste: "Ham Radio," "Vacationland (This place, this bearer of the chilly winter
burst")
Many Mountains Moving: "Celebrity"
Painted Bride Quarterly: "Lawrence Welk Dies"
Passages North: "Aerialist," "Self-Portrait with Transgression," "Synonym,"
    "Vacationland [The Vacationland Motel's swimming pool is filled]"
Perihelion: "Burn, Burn"
Permafrost: "Snow Meridian"
Pleiades: "Still Life with Half of Walter Mitty"
Ploughshares: "Sonnet: Notes from X Which Might Turn Out to Be an Elegy,
    Stemming from the U.S. Mail"
Post Road: "Excision"
Red Mouintain Review: "Approximation," "Elegy for Luggage," "Vacationland (What
    does doing it accomplish, this morning's)"
Salt Hill: "Moving through Ether"
Slope: "A Brief Elegy for Teeth," "Commiserate," "Inventory Elegy 1," "Salt"
The Southeast Review: "I Am Getting Serious About Grief"
Washington Square: "Implied Love Poem"
West Branch: "Post-Mortem Party Trick"